The Proposal

in Royal Language

Copyright © 2019 Bliss Publishing, a division of Global Celebration

All rights reserved. This book or any portion thereof may not be reproduced or used in any manner whatsoever, stored in a retrieval system, or transmitted in any form without the express written permission of the publisher, except for the use of brief quotations in a book review.

Inspired language for this mystical romance is drawn from the author's vast collection of Bible translations, especially including *The Message*, *The Passion Translation* and the cherished *King James Version* of the Holy Bible.

Printed in the United States of America.

ISBN 978-0-9963117-6-2

Designers: Cóco Banov and Caleb Durham
Illustrators: Caleb Durham, Samuil Stoyanov and Hristina Petrova
Editors: Georgian Banov and Karen Vangor

www.GlobalCelebration.com

The Proposal

in Royal Language

Winnie *Coco* Banov

Bliss Publishing, a division of Global Celebration

First Edition

IV

dedications

To my Heavenly Bridegroom,
who rescued me from this present evil world.

To my earthly Bridegroom, Georgie,
who makes it possible for us to believe together.

acknowledgments

Thank you first of all to Jesus, the Word made flesh.
You are my daily feast.

To Georgian, my protecting husband, who made it possible
for me to spend countless hours collecting the evidence,
the handfuls that have been left for us on purpose.
We discovered this treasure together.

To my colleagues in the presentation of this story,
Caleb Durham and Karen Vangor.

VIII

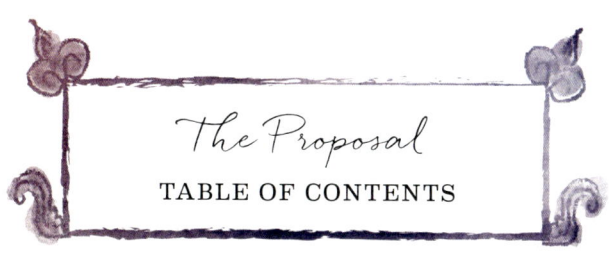

TABLE OF CONTENTS

Foreword: *Heidi Baker*	XI
Prelude: *A Word About "Co-"*	XV

Act I — 1

The Proposal	2
The Fall	10
Jehovah Desires Restoration	16
The Serenade	28
He Standeth Behind Our Wall	34

Act II — 41

Many Voices	42
The Romance of Romans	52
Romance Six	62
Romance Seven	68
The Bridge	76
Ravishing of the Heart	84
Romance Eight	92

Act III — 99

The Captivity of the Bride	100
The Song of Rescue	112
Wine at the Wedding	120

Conclusion — 131

X

foreword
by Heidi Baker

The Proposal by Winnie Cóco Banov is a tale of epic love. But this is no fairy tale, it is the true story of Christ's love for His Bride. It is a story of union, love, and pursuit. Your Bridegroom is passionately pursuing you, longing for all of your heart, and calling out your name. He wants you to give everything within you to Him. It is an exchange—your life for His. The miracle of this process is that when you die, you truly live. When you surrender all, you get pure and perfect love, not human love that fades and falters, but holy eternal love. Jesus is Love, and He is your Bridegroom. He gave Himself for your sake, for the sake of His people Israel, and for the nations. He is ready to embrace all those who call upon His name with His salvation, forgiveness, and freedom. Your past is washed away and your future is bright—He shines His light upon you.

Cóco is a dear friend of mine, and she has wholeheartedly cried out *YES!* to the King of her heart, Jesus. She lives in the joy and laughter of a young Bride fully captivated by her Lover. She didn't just read the words of life, but she said yes to the Covenant offered in the Book.

She fell in love with the Scriptures and studies a multitude of translations to clearly hear the heart of God. Just like the woman in *Song of Songs*, she wants everyone to know the One her heart loves.

Cóco did not always understand this revelation. There were years of her life when she struggled with sadness, not knowing the fullness of love. Then, the Lord wooed her deeper—"Come away with me, Beloved!" She said yes again and again to live inside His heart. She surrendered everything to Love, and there in that place of letting Him take her pain (which He had already paid for), she was able to trade her mourning for endless joy. It is too glorious not to share! Now she wants everyone to know this Love, and to laugh, dance, sing, and rejoice with her!

As you read, it will become obvious why her name is Cóco. In *The Proposal*, she writes from the revelation of "co-" as found in the ancient Greek biblical language. This prefix indicates and proves our union with Christ. We have been co-crucified, co-buried, and co-raised with Christ in the closest possible union. For a deeper study into union language, see *Love Notes,* the companion to *The Proposal*. It will change you forever. Cóco weaves *Romans* and *Song of Songs* together to lead us through this love journey. She is a scholar of the Word of God, and it is a gift to learn from her.

Love Himself comes for His Bride, giving His very life for hers. She wants to say yes, but the enemy condemns her and she forgets who she really is. He comes to win her heart again, wash her free from all her sin, and seat her at the wedding feast of freedom.

We all go through moments where we forget who we are, we forget that because Christ died, we are set free. We no longer have to live in the bondage of sin and condemnation! We no longer need to listen to those voices in our heads saying we are not good enough.

Read this love story and let Jesus carry you out of the desert leaning on your Beloved. Let Him woo you into a deeper place of revelation of union. If you want to understand the beauty and the passion of God's love for His Bride (you!), lose yourself in the pages of this love story. Let it soak deeply into your heart. Do not just skim through these pages, but be saturated in them.

I too have been won by Love. When I was 16, the Lord kissed my hand and oil ran down. That day felt like my wedding day, *and I was never the same*. Cóco and I have a special friendship because we both understand the depths of love we received as a free gift. We both live in gratitude and wonder, captivated by our Bridegroom King. Some may think this is just for certain people, but God wants everyone to know His love in this intimate way. He wants you to dance with Him and let His love wash away every bit of pain you may have endured. He does not promise a life of perfection with no problems or trials; instead, He promises to walk with you through every fire. He promises to never leave you or forsake you. All you need to do is trust that He is good, trust that He is for you. Will you let Him in? He is ready, and the depths of His love are beyond all you could ask or imagine... *Come live in His heart.*

Dr. Heidi G. Baker
Co-Founder and Executive COB of Iris Global

prelude

A Word About "Co-"

"Co-," this small prefix found in the written Word of God is from the ancient Greek language. It reveals proof of our union with Christ.

We have been co-crucified, co-buried, and co-raised with Christ in the closest possible union. It is breathtaking, stunning, beyond our dreams. *Union with Christ, here and now!* We have been drawn by cords of love.

We believe His finished work.

"Co-"

"Co-" transported me to a place, a realm,
where everything became easy.

I entered His rest.
I entered His sabbath.
Lord of Sabbath.

All striving ceased—
it was no longer necessary.

I was eclipsed, engulfed, by Him.

His grand, majestic death
had accomplished all.

My awestruck heart was still beating,
I was still breathing,
there was still breath in my lungs;
my eyes were wide open—
beholding the crucified One.

The brazen Serpent on the pole,
The smitten Shepherd,
The bruised One.

I saw Him high and lifted up
and at the same time condescending to me—
the lost orphan, afraid and hiding,
knowing what I deserved
(it wasn't this love).

"Co-"

this is my treasure.
So small, so delicate, nearly missed.

But it was my handful on purpose,
left for me to discover.

"Why me?"
I asked a thousand times.

Why not?

Then everyone will know without a doubt that it's all about Him.

No talent, dedication, ability,
perseverance on my part—

"Co-"

a Handful on Purpose, left for me.

Have you found yours?

proposal

pro·pos·al

/prəˈpōzəl/

noun—

1. the act of an offering or suggesting something for acceptance, adoption or preference

2. a plan, a scheme proposed

3. an offer or suggestion of marriage

xx

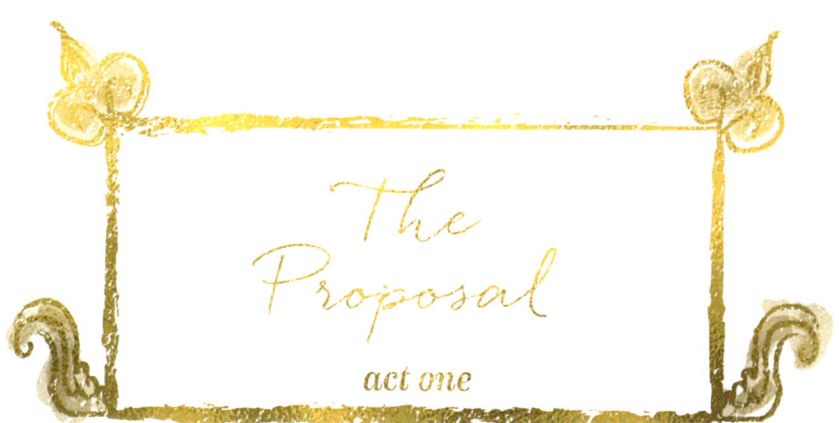

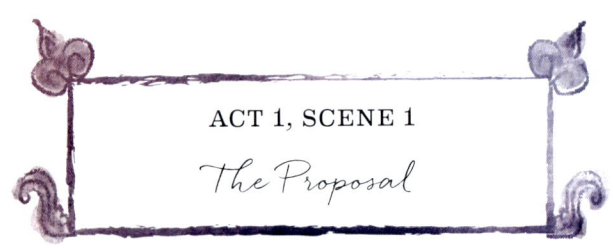

ACT 1, SCENE 1
The Proposal

This is a Proposal,

in a language sometimes hidden

and at other times

appearing in bold and brilliant

beauty before our eyes.

The Royal Language

this language of

love, union, and marriage

can be found on nearly every

page of our most sacred

document, the Holy Scripture.

*It reveals Jehovah's love for Israel,
Christ's passion for His Bride, The Church.*

The Royal Language,

the holy language of Canaan,

like golden nuggets,

can be found in unalloyed purity

within the pages of

the Song of Solomon.

And searching each page of Scripture

with your heart's affections,

amazed, you will discover

the Royal Language

lying just beneath the surface.

*These golden nuggets lead us
to unending veins of purest gold,
countless diamond mines,
and pearl-strewn sands
on the shores of God's fathomless
ocean of love.*

*The more we discover,
the more we desire to hear
and to learn this heavenly love song
sung with royal lyrics.*

*After all, it's by our words,
our expressions,
that the real thoughts and secrets
of the heart are revealed.*

We don't need to dig deep to see the
language of marriage
used to describe
Israel's relationship with Jehovah.

As evidenced in Scripture,
Israel was the wife of Jehovah,
meant to enjoy all the privileges
the Royal Marriage would provide:

love,
Tenderness,
protection,
and provision

—all for raising the
generations yet to be born
in safety and in peace.

After betrothing Israel to Himself
and entering into the marriage covenant
by the sprinkling of blood at Sinai,

she became His—
the dearly beloved of His soul.

He had found her
on the day of her birth,
abandoned and forsaken.

He washed her; He covered her nakedness,
clothing her in the finest linen
and silk, adorning her with
jewels and gold.

She became His,
famous for the beauty
and glory He had given her.

All dowry gifts became hers:

righteousness,

justice,

lovingkindness,

faithfulness.

Her Betrothed One
imparted lavish, divine gifts
upon her, and she became
flesh of His flesh and
bone of His bone.

The Two became One.

He rejoiced over her
as a Bridegroom rejoices over the Bride,
desiring that she cleave only unto Him.

She was a peculiar Treasure
above all others.

She became famous for
the exceedingly magnificent,
complete and perfect beauty with which
Jehovah had clothed her.

But with great sadness
we have a darkened image
painted before our eyes
in the first covenant.

It records the virgin Israel's history and her fall.

Marriage language serves to magnify
the intimate relationship
Jehovah had with Israel.
It describes His heartbreak and
the harsh reality of her rebellion,
as she began taking other lovers.

ACT 1, SCENE 2
The Fall

Taking pride in her own

beauty and fame,

she forgot that it was all a gift.

As Israel began taking other lovers,
she broke her marriage covenant.

Her estrangement from Jehovah

caused her to spiral

downward

in

darkness

and

isolation.

Israel, the Holy Seed, so quickly enticed

by the idols surrounding her,

began mingling herself with the

nations and learned their ways.

She began to speak another language,
a **mixed tongue**,
the language of Ashdod,
and no longer spoke
the Royal Language of Love.

She began worshiping false,
man-made gods.
She bowed the knee to Baal
and kissed the calves of gold.

*It was the deadly kiss
of betrayal.*

Her affections
turned away from Jehovah—
she had given them to others.

Her banishment was inevitable,
because now she desired to be
without her husband, Jehovah.

So with her bill of divorcement,
she was given into the hands
of her so-called lovers.

Quickly, her beauty and glory
began to fade.

The presence of Jehovah was withdrawn.

With no one to protect her,
her lovers began to
use and abuse her
until nothing was left.

She was in the hands of the enemy.

Her land was stripped,
her cities destroyed;
the Temple was robbed,
and songs of joy turned
into Lamentations.

Finally, she was taken captive
and scattered to foreign lands,
shamed and humiliated.

She became the property of another,
a slavery that no nation
or individual should ever know.

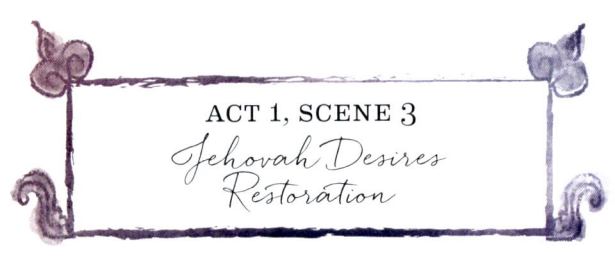

ACT 1, SCENE 3
Jehovah Desires Restoration

But all along...

Jehovah desires restoration,

The Bridegroom desires The Bride.

As we read Israel's history
we are almost dumbfounded
at Jehovah's passionate jealousy,
constantly watching over Israel
for her good,
for her beauty,
for her restoration.

Through voice after voice,
He pleads His case for her,
calling her back.
Each time is met with refusal,
yet He calls and calls again,
calls her to return to Him.

*He desires to take her back,
to take her shame away.*

He longs for her restoration.

*Jehovah, in the magnitude
of His mercy and grace,
remembers the kindness
of her youth
when she went after Him
in the wilderness.*

*The prophets were all witness to this:
her youth, her love
and her betrothal to Jehovah.*

They sang her love songs.

*But they also witnessed
her betrayal and banishment...
her exile where she lived
as a widow,
barren and fruitless,
without a husband's protection.*

Their songs continued.

*But the songs of joy turned
into songs of Lamentations
expressing grief and anguish over
her beauty that was quickly fading.*

*Forgetting Jehovah,
the fallen Bride was easily
led astray
by false prophets,
unholy priests,
and wicked kings,
who left her in a state of
complete devastation.*

Jehovah, with His eyes on her restoration,

speaks kindly and tenderly

to her heart,

He speaks the Royal Language

that longs to forgive,

to restore, to receive

her into His favor again,

to forget the past,

to set her free from all

guilt and shame.

But she has forgotten Him.

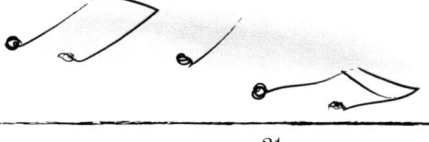

*The Father's eye is on
the long-awaited incarnation,
the body of His Son
has been prepared.
He would be given in sacrifice,
He would make full satisfaction
in the courts of Heaven.*

His eye is on the Bridegroom.

*His blood would
bathe her from
all corruption.*

But she has lost sight of Him.

The Psalmists,

the Poets,

the Prophets,

all friends of The Bridegroom,

wait with joyful anticipation

at His coming incarnation.

They lend their voices

to prepare the way.

The

Bridegroom

will

be

sacrificed

for all the world to see.

His blood

poured out,

He will be

crucified

through

weakness.

*The Bride will be restored
in the sight of all the nations.*

With awe and wonder we wait and watch

to see the Bride restored

in the glorious coming

of the New Covenant,

and the long-awaited marriage feast

that will celebrate

The Lamb and His Bride.

But she has forgotten Him.

ACT 1, SCENE 4
The Serenade

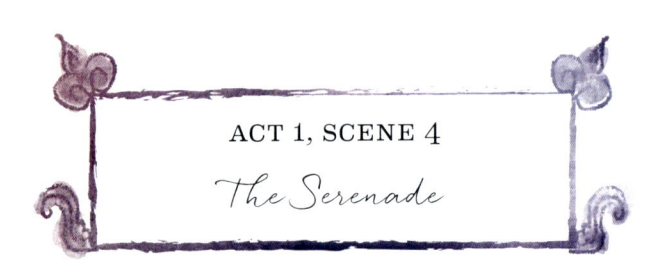

To the chief Musician

a song of Love for My Beloved

The Song of all Songs

for My Beloved

"I remember My promises...
I remember..."

With love songs He is

calling her back.

The voices of the Old Covenant

prepare the way...

The Bridegroom is coming

for His Bride.

"My tongue is the pen
of a ready writer..."

My heart is a fountain gushing with love for you
When I remember the kindness of your youth —
You went after me in the wilderness, there I will
allure you back and speak romantic and
tender words to win you back —

I remember.

I call and plead my case for you for I am your
Maker and Husband, Jehovah with everlasting
mercies I will have you back — I desire to take
away the shame of your youth and the Barrenness of
your Widowhood and for you to live under
the Shadow of my wings,
my protection, my love, my dove,
my beautiful One, my
undefiled, My Bride.
I desire you — my love,
my love, my love

*I, Jehovah, your Husband,
remember the kindness of your youth
when you went after Me
in the wilderness.*

*I remember your youthful loyalty,
our love as newlyweds!*

*There I will allure you
again, speaking
romantic and tender
words to win you back.*

*I call and plead My
case with you,
for I am your Maker
and your Husband.*

With everlasting mercies,
I will have you back!

I desire to take the shame
of your widowhood away.

I desire for you to live
under the wings
of my protection.

ACT 1, SCENE 5
He Standeth Behind our Wall

*Before
faith came and before
His appearing He shewed Himself
through the lattice. Some could only
catch a glimpse of Him and His beauty,
while others, with eyes opened by faith,
could gaze on the Bridegroom,
their hearts' affections being
stirred as they waited in faith for
His full manifestation, His incarnation.*

> Behold,
> He standeth behind
> our wall,
> He looketh forth at
> the windows,
> showing Himself
> through the lattice.
>
> *Song of Songs 2:9*

But who has believed our report?

To most, He looked like a
root out of dry ground,
with neither form nor magnificence,
without beauty—

"There was nothing we saw
that would make us desire Him."

*But soon the Father
will show Him openly displayed
on the Cross.*

The Proposal

act two

ACT 2, SCENE 1
Many Voices

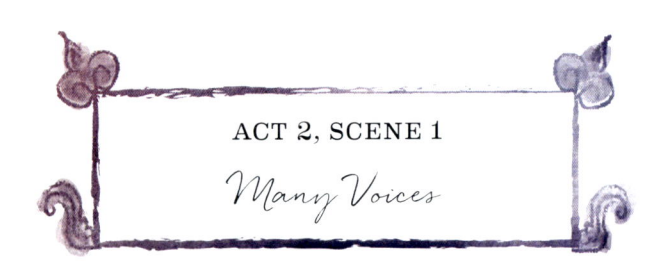

*The Bridegroom
appeared in a form like ours
and began to call forth His Bride.*

Enemies appeared also—
unbelievers and workers of darkness
with murderous spirits.

*As His name began to be poured out
like fragrant oil,
the multitudes followed.*

—but so did His enemies.
Spirits of jealousy and envy arose
and began their deadly plot.
This plot was nothing new.

His enemies' voices had sung their own song
 from the very beginning,
a song both discordant and hopeless.

The alluring voice
 of deception in the garden,
the fiery voice of idolatry,
 enslaving the people who had
just been freed.

The filthy voice of accusation,
 sounding day and night,
their song crescendoed.

Their vision focused,
 their sights now set on Him.

 Like a pack of ravenous wolves,
they descended on the Lamb.

*But all along,
the Lamb has been looking for
and calling out to His Bride.*

John the Baptist,
friend of the Bridegroom,
was the first voice to announce
He was the Lamb of God.

His joy was made full
as he heard the voice of the Bridegroom
calling for His Bride.

The Lamb's voice of love
speaking the Royal Language
began to awaken
sleeping hearts.

No one ever spoke like This —
His words were words of life.

All were being called
to the marriage supper of the Lamb.

More and more continued to
follow this Man of Love,
losing sight of their everyday cares.

As the enemies of the Bridegroom
watched the multitudes,
their jealousy increased
and they became inflamed with rage.

They planned to kill Him,
yet they feared the crowds.

But they were determined to find a way,
and continued to close in on their prey.

Those betrothed to the Bridegroom
enjoyed His company
for many days,
and at a final meal with Him,
He pledged His life for them.

As His last three days began to unfold,
some were confused,
others were frightened,
as they sensed the danger
that hung in the air.

While John the Beloved

affectionately leaned on his Beloved,

he received a ravishing vision.

Soon he would pen what he saw:
The Bride adorned for her Husband.

"Look! It's the Bride,

the wife of the Lamb."

The enemies' plan was formed—
one of His own would betray Him,
the kiss of betrayal, cold and cruel.

The Bridegroom was sold
for 30 pieces of silver—
arrested, bound like Isaac,
and led away.

He was falsely accused, bruised and beaten,
slapped, spit upon, and mocked
as they plucked His beard.

His body quivering from the scourging,
He was crowned with thorns and robed in scarlet,
humiliated as He was presented to the world.

Ecce Homo!
Behold the Man!

Yet He opened not His mouth as He was unjustly tried—
a mistrial that quickly sentenced Him
to the horror and cruelty of
death by crucifixion.

No one knew
this was the plan of His Father.

"Strike the Shepherd
and the sheep will scatter."

Many sneered at Him,
as He was lifted up for all the world to see.

As He breathed His last breath,

He called out, "Kalah!"

"My Bride!"

and gave His spirit into

the hands of His Father.

A handful of frightened

and trembling betrothed ones looked on.

They were His witnesses.

He was buried and the tomb was sealed.

*For three dark days
there was silence in Heaven,
a thundering silence
that echoed in His grave.*

And then it happened—
the great High Priest
after the order of Melchizedek
was raised from the dead.

He was alive!

They saw Him,
spoke with Him,
ate with Him,
Touched His wounds.

Rivers of Joy
overflowed as they received
what He and the Father had promised:
His Holy Spirit indwelling humanity,
the pouring out of the "New Wine."

Now the world must know.

ACT 2, SCENE 2
The Romance of Romans

Paul, once an enemy, now a lover,

like no other psalmist of

the New Covenant,

has penned the lyrics

of this astonishing, romantic love song,

so strong and brilliant.

Paul has captured the love wine

being poured out,

as it burst forth from

the Spirit on the day

the promise was fulfilled.

It is the song of the Lamb
which expresses the
thoughts and the secrets
of the Bridegroom's heart.

*It is the song of union
with His Beloved Bride.*

It is the romance of Romans.

A passionate and jealous friend
of the Bridegroom,
Paul still guards the Church today,
warning her what will happen
if she listens to a stranger's voice.

His desire is to present her
as a chaste virgin
to one husband,
Christ, the Beloved.

With breathtaking language
he distilled the romance
of Solomon's Song
"I am my Beloved's and He is mine"
into a new reality of union.

Christ the Bridegroom
has come to make us one
with Himself, here and now.

You are His Bride!

Let this love song,
this song of the marriage of the Lamb,
dwell in your hearts richly.

It will inhabit your being,
spilling out of the heart's deepest fountain
in hymns, melodies, serenades,
and spiritual songs with Royal Language,
the melody becoming sweeter and sweeter
every time you hear it.

Hear it,
believe it,
learn it,
sing it.

It is the Song of all Songs,
the union of Christ
with the believer.

The Song of Songs,

penned by King Solomon,

was the most excellent song of all.

This song is being sung over you, here and now—

it's about your union with the Bridegroom.

*Paul's love letters are serenades
revealing The Lamb.*

Though crucified in weakness,

Christ is the Resurrected One,

the One "Greater than Solomon."

A word about union:

*Among the thousands of words
translated in the Scripture,
too few adequately
express the essence of*
*Christ the Beloved's death
and our participation with Him in it,*
*resulting in a living union with the Resurrected One,
the bliss of Heaven on earth!*

*This union is the gift of grace
received with childlike faith.*

*The words that clearly express
union are found lying
just beneath the surface.*

*Like lost, buried treasures,
they are now discovered
and displayed in public
for all to see.*

*These treasured words
without doubt
reveal to you, His Bride,
your union with Christ
here and now,
because His work is finished!*

In the ancient Greek language,
we discovered a small (almost unnoticed,
but extremely significant) prefix.

"co-"

It is a primary preposition
that denotes union,
the closest of all possible unions.

This union

—of close, personal belonging to Christ—

inflamed Paul's heart

with Heaven's passion.

Throughout his love letters,

Paul gently but continuously reminds the Bride

and leads her into this revelation...

being co-crucified with Christ is just the beginning.

Let us fall into

the romance of Romans,

sung by the apostle Paul,

and be caught

in the divine love net

woven with gold and glory.

Let us sing

the Royal Language

of the Cross.

Let the revelation of union

with Christ the Bridegroom

be yours!

ACT 2, SCENE 3
Romance 6
Evidence of Union

Rise up,
my love, my fair one
and come away.

Rejoice, O barren one...

With great passion

He, the Bridegroom,

desired to eat the Passover meal

and to accomplish

His work on the Cross.

And in an unparalleled victory,

He put an end

to death and the grave.

His Bride was the Joy set before Him.

Embraced in His loving arms,
He takes us with Him
in His finished work.

He suffered, He bled, He died,
He was buried,
and He took us with Him.

Union with Christ the Beloved
is now expressed,
"with Christ I have been
co-crucified,
co-buried, and
co-raised."

"I am my Beloved's and
He is mine."
His desire is towards me.

Selah.

And now we've been given
His wonderful new life
to share and enjoy.

All the voices from the
New Covenant
sing this serenade
for The Bride of Christ.

She echoes, "I do."

They invite all to belong
to this one Husband
and to be present at the
marriage supper of the Lamb
as His Bride.

The new everlasting covenant
speaking in Royal Language
calls you to be

Married To Another

to belong to Christ,
to rest under His banner of Love
and to hear Him call you
His Beloved.

Union with Christ
produces fruit for God,
fruit unto holiness.

Abiding in Christ,
vine and branch,
brings forth this fruit.

This is a great mystery.

Christ the Beloved
and the Church,
two becoming one
in Marriage Union.

ACT 2, SCENE 4
Romance 7:1-4
Evidence of Marriage

Having died with Christ,

you will find yourself

in a new Royal Domain,

now free to be

married to Another.

For your Maker is your Husband.

You are united,

you do belong,

you are joined,

to Him who rose from the dead.

And you are free
to give yourself
in marriage, so to speak,
to Another.

You have found yourself
Another Husband
in Him who rose from the dead.

You are truly free to marry
a resurrection life
and bear fruit for God
with no condemnation.

Christ the Beloved
became cursed beyond measure

so that you could be lawfully

married to Another,

to Him who rose from the dead.

What God has joined together
(yoked together, conjoined in marriage)
let no man put asunder
(place room between, separate, divide, or divorce).

Take this, my yoke, upon you.

It is easy. It is light.

The believer that is

joined to the Lord

is one spirit with Him,

a mystical marriage

between the believer and Christ.

The Bride's spirit is united

with the Spirit of Christ

and she is one with Him

in faith and love.

Christ and His Bride have one will.

*Yoked together,
she is happily ruled, governed, and protected
by her Beloved.*

*She is no longer unequally yoked
with the world, but is
supernaturally yoked by faith
with Christ the Beloved,
the Husband,
in perfect partnership.*

*The Bride has been adorned
for her Husband.*

*She is His perfect partner,
His friend,
His Bride.*

The Bride and Bridegroom in union,

she is made complete,

dressed in His Righteousness

(He counts it as her own).

Purified from within by His

outpoured blood,

She is given a new language.

It is the pure, Royal Language

that speaks of

His finished work on the Cross.

He acted as the Spouse

in lifting her up

in the Divine Rescue

to be His Bride

for all eternity.

Set me as a seal upon your heart,

because love is stronger than death.

The flood of sin can not drown this love.

Hear the song He is singing over you, His Bride.

Will you say *yes* to His proposal?

ACT 2, SCENE 5
The Bridge

His serenade carries you over the treacherous

waters, bringing you safely to the other side.

the bridge of a song

bridge /brij/

noun—a musical term

- a unique passage that *breathes life* into the music
- it provides a new melody
- it takes the song in a *new direction*
- fragile and delicate in nature
- a lyrical micro-diary, *a plot twist in the song*
- a place to pause and reflect on earlier portions of the song
- a transition that heightens the emotional level

The Song of Songs

Who is this coming up out of the Wilderness

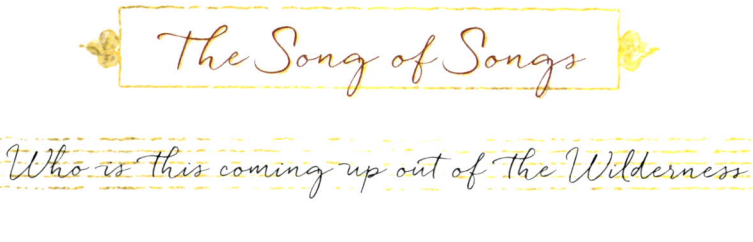

leaning on her Beloved? She is the

Royal Companion of the Prince of Life.

Who is this coming up out of the Wilderness,

like pillars of smoke, perfumed with myrrh and

frankincense, with all powders of the merchants?

It is the One who is "Greater than Solomon"

and His Ransomed Bride!

The beloved Bridegroom condescended from on high and stooped to lift her up.

He gave His life for her.

Now He lifts her up and she leans on Him, no longer trusting in her own ways.

From the attar of her heart, perfumes rise

for all to see: frankincense, myrrh,

spices and powders of the merchants,

cleansing and purifying.

The bloodwashed Bride & her Bridegroom.

Who is this coming up out of the Wilderness,

leaning on her Beloved?

She is lifted up — taken out of the wilderness

leaning on her Beloved,

she is no longer alone.

She is the Royal Companion

of the Prince of life.

She has been drawn by cords of Love.

ACT 2, SCENE 6
Ravishing of the Heart

Now that Christ the Beloved

has come

He is no longer hiding

in the shadows

or behind the veil.

He has been given to us

in His fullest passion.

"You have ravished my heart,

my sister, my spouse.

"How fair is thy love,

my sister, my spouse.

"I am come into my garden,

my sister, my spouse."

Now that He has come

we have been given new eyes,

dove's eyes

that see Him by faith,

constantly beholding

His grace and beauty.

The veil is torn forever,
now we see Him
in His finished work.

We, with dove's eyes,

see His blood poured out.

We see Him

displayed on the tree.

We see Him high

and lifted up.

The Bride sees The Bridegroom.

She sees the

price He paid.

She sees union

with Him.

Her heart is

ravished.

He acted as a Spouse

in lifting her up.

He has loved her

as a Spouse.

She has ravished

His heart.

He said,

"Behold my hands,

Behold my feet,

Behold my side."

Her eyes are closed

to all others but Him.

She has dove's eyes.

She sees His wounds.

Now that Christ has come,
There is no condemnation
for those who belong to Christ,
for those who are joined
in life-union with the Beloved.

There is no judgment,
no guilt, no shame,
because she is joined
to Him by faith and love.

She is married to Another,
even to Him who was
raised from the dead.

He betrothed Himself to her
to take away her shame.

She sings, ♪♪
"I am my Beloved's
and He is mine."

He acted as a Spouse;

He loved her as a Spouse.

He lifted her up and

       took her shame away.

And you, whose heart has been

ravished by His love,

will not be ashamed,

nor insulted,

nor confounded,

nor humiliated,

nor dishonored.

You will not be reproached.

You will forget the shame
of your youth,
and will not remember
the disgrace of your widowhood.

For your Maker is your Husband,
who has given Himself to you.

The winter is over and gone,
the time of the singing
of birds is come.

It is finished, my Bride!
There is no condemnation!
I have taken it away.

ACT 2, SCENE 7
Romance 8
The Greatest Mystery of All

Let us not forget His death

(and ours)

released us from our former

lovers so we could be...

Married to Another
To Him who was
raised from the dead.

Christ the Beloved became cursed

beyond measure

so we could live in bliss

beyond measure,

married to Another.

*There is therefore no charge outstanding
against those who are in
wedlock to Jesus Christ.*

*There can be no condemnation
to those who are in union with Christ.
For He took all the condemnation
on Himself on the tree.*

*Listen to the treasured Royal Language
used to express our love-union with our Bridegroom.*

*His death (and ours) released us
from all other lovers;
therefore, there is
no condemnation
to those who are in
life-union with Christ,
the Beloved.*

*We are honorably
married to Another,
even to Him who was
raised from the dead.*

*The power of His love alone
accomplished all this.*

Enjoying the Bridegroom's presence,

we are now set

as a seal on His arm,

as a seal on His heart.

This love is stronger than death,

this love outlasts the grave,

and triumphs over all!

He is pouring the new wine of His love

into the new wineskin

of our new heart.

He has pledged

to never leave us,

never forsake us,

and never divorce us.

Therefore there is no condemnation

for those who are in

Marriage Union with Christ

the Beloved.

Wherefore they are no more 2,
but 1 flesh.

Love Wine Outpoured
Love that is stronger than death
Marriage Union   Life Union
Our joined death raised us
into eternal wedlock
with our Beloved.
Married to
Another

What God has joined together
(yoked together, conjoined in marriage)
let no man put asunder
(place room between, separate, divide, or divorce).

The Proposal

act three

Taking us back in time,
the Apostle Paul remembers how it was
before the Bridegroom was revealed,
and gives warning to the young Bride.

The strange voices of the accusers will come...
Don't lose sight of the Crucified One.

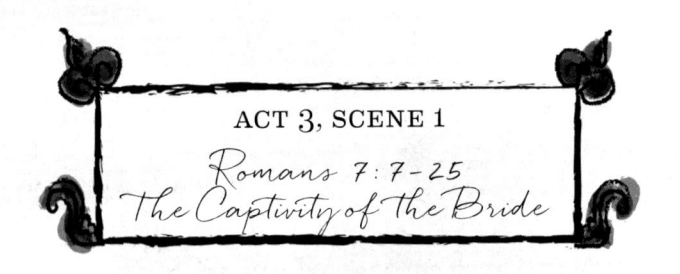

ACT 3, SCENE 1
Romans 7:7-25
The Captivity of the Bride

Advances from the enemies—accusations to the young Bride challenge her. Their voices are strange, but she desires to please them all.

And so she listens.

"How is it possible to live continually in the bliss and ecstasy of first love?" the enemies of the Cross demandingly ask.

"You boast that you are the Bride of the King, making yourself royalty. That is quite a claim! We know where you come from.

"You say you are dressed in a beautiful white wedding gown. All we see are your old, filthy rags."

Voice after voice, little by little, she loses sight of her Royal identity and finds herself caught between two opinions.

Disharmony and estrangement hang heavy in the atmosphere that was once filled with joy and love songs.

The Bride is losing sight of her first love. The bewitchment and seduction has begun, as she is slowly led away from the glorious banner of love under which she once lived.

She is no longer speaking the Royal Language and begins to speak a *mixed tongue* (the language of the adversary).

The trap is set.
She is lured into the the snare.
The treacherous affair has begun.

The Law was witness to all of this.
It was her guardian,
given to guide her until the Incarnation.
She was to live her life devoted,
in faith and love (these were the keys to promised freedom,
that would keep her safe).

But the Seducer, lurking in every shadow,
quickly moved in, casting doubt and heaping on demands.

Wasn't she required to obey the rules in strict perfection?

Taking her eyes off her Beloved,
the only thing the young Bride could see
was her own failure.

Feeling alone,
all she was able to produce was distorted and rotten...
fruit unto death.

Trapped behind bars of accusation and guilt,
freedom seemed more and more impossible
with each impending
failure.

As time went on, she bore no good fruit.
With nothing to show but miscarriages and stillbirths,
she was shackled to this domineering mate of Sin.*

**Romans 7:5, The Message*

Now caught between two deadly forces,
she was co-habiting with Sin and Evil
and nothing good was being produced.

She was taken captive, a prisoner,
held in bondage and slavery.

Her seducer had become her slave master.

Beguiled, she was sold—
trafficked as a piece of merchandise
to be used and finally disposed of.

This was a slavery that no one should ever know.

Selfie *Personal Brand*

Man Pleasing Spirit

Social Media Persona

Dying Daily

Captivity

Perpetual Warfare

Could this
false persona of Sin
be the slave master,
the Old Man
playing the role of an
abusive mate?

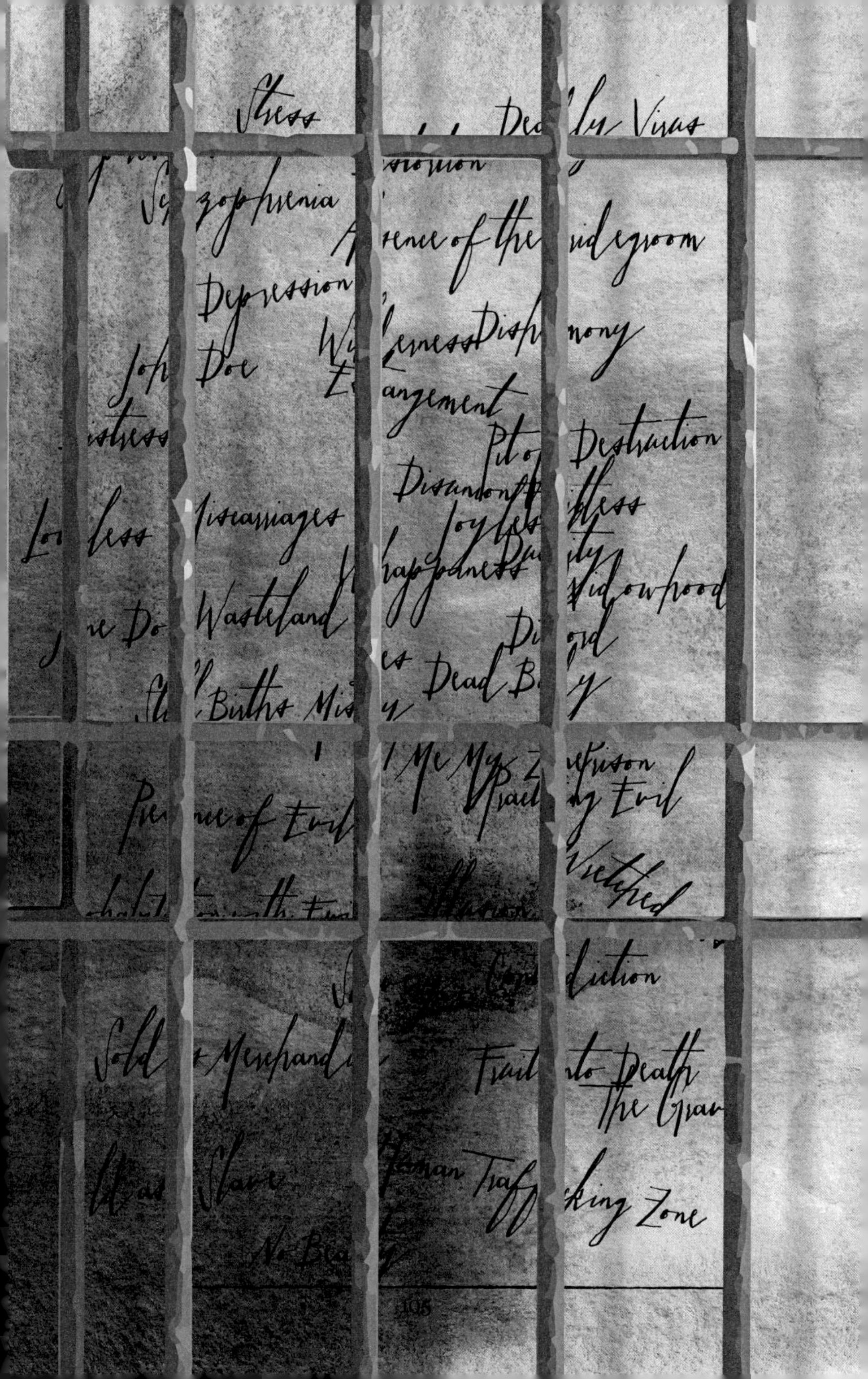
Stress
Depression
John Doe
Wasteland
Destruction
Zone

Oh Wretched One that I am! Who can rescue me?

The language
found in Romans 7:7-25
undeniably displays
our former relationship with
the false persona of Sin.

This is the wretched
condition from which
the Bride needs to be rescued.

Let us be clear,
once and for all,
concerning our Beloved
and His finished work.

Let us be clear about the captivity that He rescued us from.

Is it possible to be
Married to Another,
to Him who rose from the dead,
and to be in
slavery and bondage
to the false persona of Sin and Evil
at the same time?

The Bridegroom will not
leave His Bride in this
broken condition
trapped by lies and illusions.

Oh wretched one
that I am!

I am the one caught between two opinions.

Who can rescue me from this bewitchment?

The cry of the distressed one reached His ears.

The Divine Rescue already accomplished,

He lifts you up, His blood-washed Bride.

"Out of the grave came a song!"

ACT 3, SCENE 2
The Song of Rescue

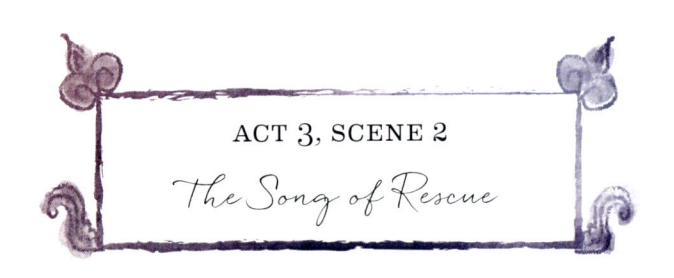

The voice of my Beloved,
"Open to me my sister,
my spouse, my love,
my undefiled."

The Beloved speaks

and you hear that voice.

"My Bride, My Sister,

My Spouse."

With His voice,
He rescues you
from all other lovers.

He forgives,

He washes,

He restores.

Now Faith has come.

You watch Him

as He writes a love note in the sand

"You belong to Me.

I take your judgment,

your condemnation,

your punishment.

I take your deadness."

"You belong To Me!"

And with that,

He displayed redemption

and taught the world

The Royal Language of Love.

Behold the blood-washed Bride!

*The Law has been fulfilled by Another
and you have been pronounced pure and clean.*

Fainting with love,

you find yourself

suddenly "transported to His house of wine."

Leaning on your Beloved,

you are coming up out of the wilderness.

The "greater than Solomon" is here.

And you,

the Bride of Christ,

the Wife of the Lamb,

are fairer than

Solomon's Shulamite.

Now you know

your new identity.

He has given you
His own name.

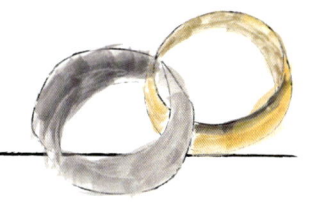

ACT 3, SCENE 3
Wine at the Wedding

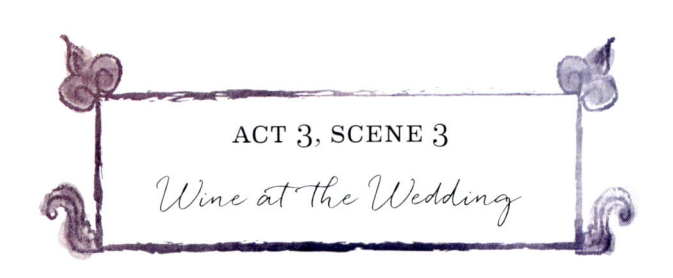

The Bride remembered...

When the wine at the
wedding of Cana ran out,
the Heavenly Bridegroom
(in disguise)
turned ordinary water into
wine and poured it out.

It was called by those who
tasted it, the best wine,
the most valuable and
beautiful wine of all.

"His love is better than wine."

Then suddenly, He transported me to His house of wine!

All the serenading, minstrel voices
of the new covenant
call you to join in
the marriage supper
of the Lamb
and be co-seated
with the Bridegroom.

The beauty of the restoration is upon us.

The Bridegroom poured
out His blood.

Bliss, the ecstasy of salvation,
can be found here and now
upon receiving this
unspeakable gift.

The spotless Lamb of God
has been given for
the Bride.

*The wine now pouring,
the wedding celebration
has begun!*

*It is the open espousal of
the Bride and the
Bridegroom, the gift
from the Father
to the Son.*

Those who belong to Christ...

Christ the Beloved now has her

as His own possession,

not only in His arms

to have and to hold,

but in His heart,

from where she can

never be plucked.

*What God has joined together
let no man put asunder.*

He has betrothed Himself to her forever, for all eternity, and the marriage supper of the Lamb is the public celebration.

And for those enjoying the Bridegroom's presence they find it impossible
　　　To fast,
　　　　To mourn,
　　　　　To weep.

All the affections of her heart, soul, and mind

are caught up and melted into

the Heavenly Bridegroom's heart.

Listen to the love song,

the serenade,

that He is

singing over you.

*He is rejoicing over His Bride
and all who hear His voice rejoice.*

He is ravished by the

communion and company

of His Bride.

Come...

eat and drink

abundantly,

oh Beloved.

He saved the best wine for now!

...Suddenly transported

to His House of Wine!

Christ's death provides it all:
forgiveness, cleansing, freedom,
release from bondage and the tyranny of Sin,
victory, and everlasting joy.

Married to Another is the reason for no condemnation!

This is a proposal, based on love alone,
offered in mercy and grace, from the Lover of your Soul.

This is my Beloved, this is my friend,
Yes, He is altogether lovely.

The Proposal
conclusion

Does this all

sound like a dream?

A fairy tale,
Too good to be true?

A story someone just made up?

Does this story end

happily ever after?

*These are the questions that
stir the deepest part of the heart.*

Who has the answers that truly satisfy?

*The answers could be very close,
lying just beneath the surface
like buried treasure.*

*Perhaps we should reconsider
His proposal.*

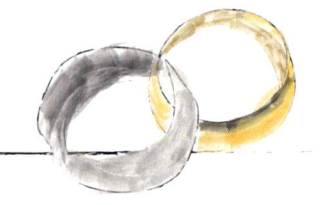

We have unearthed some of these buried treasures and present them in

Love Notes
A Companion to
The Proposal

This is a deep study of the book of Romans giving you scriptural evidence that invites you to daily experience marriage union and intimacy with Christ, our Beloved Bridegroom.

In all of Scripture, one of the most significant and notable themes is marriage. This study guide of Romans 6, 7, and 8, viewed exclusively through the lens of marriage language, will help unravel the "theological knot" of the New Testament (Romans 7:5-25). It will help you identify all of the language that points to the believer's union with Christ here and now. Chapter topics include:

1. **The Prelude:** Interpreting Romans through the language of marriage.

2. **Evidence of Union:** Discovering, from the Greek language, a buried treasure that reveals our union with Christ.

3. **Evidence of Marriage:** Israel and Jehovah, Christ and His Bride. Going from the shadow of the Old Covenant to the living reality of the New.

4. **The Greatest Mystery of All:** Belonging to Christ—two becoming one.

5. **A Most Treacherous Affair:** Who is this Romans 7 Man vying for our affections?

6. **The Marriage Bridge:** Taking us in a new direction, this is a song of love and rescue.

My prayer for you is that you allow these treasures to become planted forever in your heart, like seeds that will reap an abundant harvest. God wants to give you heart-flaming proof from Scripture of your absolute freedom from the tyranny of Sin and your everlasting, indissolvable union with the Lover of your soul, Jesus Christ.

You are no longer alone, stranded in a wilderness season, or left to fight through a life of daily struggle. Your dreams of intimacy with God are no longer just a faint, flickering flame. He is inviting you to His banqueting table, where He is celebrating and singing over you.

Blood-washed and forgiven, you are part of this story because you are married to Another. You are now invited to partake of the wedding feast.

I pray that this story has awakened your heart and your appetite. Are you ready for a second course?

Visit this link to download an exclusive taste of Love Notes:
www.globalcelebration.com/love-notes-appetizer
and enter the password FEAST

Wedding Feast Menu

The Master Chef
highly recommends that
these two offerings on today's menu
The Proposal and *Love Notes*
be consumed together.

The love wine of *The Proposal* pairs excellently
with the main course found in *Love Notes*.

Eat and drink of this love feast and enter into the
enjoyment of your marriage union with Jesus.

It's what He died for.

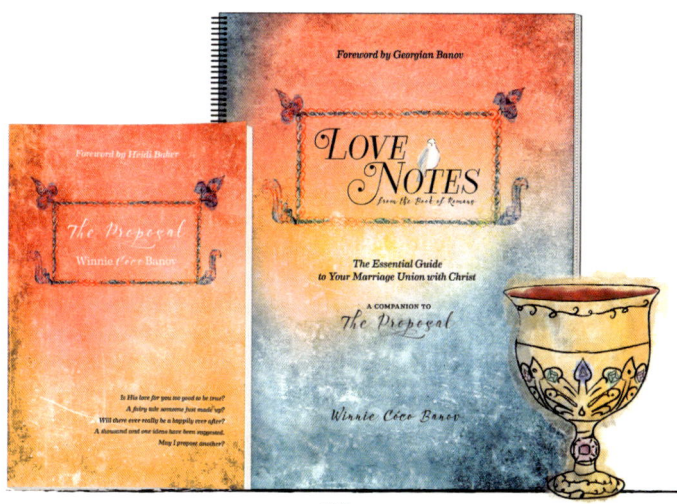

Will you accept His proposal?

Tutto Finito!
It is Finished!

Love Notes